THE EPHEMERAL AGE

BY

BYRON RIZZO

PREFACE

Nothing in this world or universe is alien to change. Change as an infinitesimal constant, from the great cosmic spheres, to our own bodies and their cellular dimension, affects everything that exists. Even if the dynamic is too big to be noticed, it is there. Due to strange paradoxes of the mind, the human beings, inserted in so much constant metamorphosis, nevertheless usually have their qualms to accept or feel comfortable in such an inevitable transformation. From the ancient dogmas that are in charge of maintaining traditions, to the great philosophical movements that are always in force, or the same location of the settlements that has been repeated for centuries, we have a marked custom for what is known.

Perhaps for this very reason the transformations that we have been undergoing since the end of the Middle Ages, more precisely since the Discovery of America and the invention of the Printing Press, created a series of new characteristic paradigms, unknown until then. Never so fast and with the force of an indomitable whirlpool, than in the last 100 years. The massiveness of electric power, the end of various political paths, 2 World Wars, the heyday of arts and media such as radio and television, as well as faster and more efficient forms of physical transportation. Explosions of change that we have not yet fully understood, and that are and will be the subject of study in the centuries to come.

The greatest catalyst for differences, the largest variable that created others and produced an irreconcilable schism with the past, came however in the last 30 years. Because if there was something that, when everything seemed to be already invented, gave it a new meaning, reconverted it, and even made obsolete the previous forms of interaction, it was the Internet.

We will never be able to realize ourselves, the impact that the great network of networks has had on the culture, the way of consuming information, of working and relating. It is very likely that in the decades that await us, only the new generations, who did not live in the world that until so recently was the common, the known, the immovable, could assess its real weight. We, immersed in change, in constant adaptation, riding the wave, have the protagonist's perspective. It may take some spectator from a distance to notice how far and to which point we are moving right now. Even the accelerated, stumbled and never more present changes that the Internet is undergoing. Because even this is not alien to the infinite metamorphosis that the humans must go through and imprints on every thing that they create.

Beyond the stages that can be easily differentiated, those that conglomerate large periods of time such as the so-called Internet 1.0 and 2.0, day by day, month by month, year by year, our magical electrical network mutates. Applications are born, markets, forums and pages are launched, just as many others disappear. Transformation is the law, however, not everything survives or has an equivalent that succeeds it. In the same way that happens with evolution in other, more biological planes, there are species and particularities that become extinct, are lost, or their essence is so disrupted that it is not possible to recognize the same entity.

The vast majority of people do not know and have no reason to know, but what they see as eternalized on the web, could not be further from that assessment. In fact, the fragility of the online is so huge, that it is enough for its servers to stop having maintenance to make it disappear. Everything we see there is backed up in several places, in addition to having someone in care, a guardian for all legal purposes, but also with the responsibility of repairing errors, uploading things again. Everything on the Internet, then, is kept alive through a behind-the-scenes effort. In the absence of it, things start to fail, the standards change and nobody adapts the pages or applications to them, and in case of not renewing the subscription to the server, or that the provider of the same stops giving it; there all traces disappear.

Humanity and its means of perpetuating itself have always been particularly fragile. More times than we would like to admit, because of mistakes, political conflicts or natural disasters bigger than us. Immense amounts of culture and history have had to be assumed, deduced, calculated, due the lack of reliable written or oral reference. We are not only talking about past times hidden from the historical light, thousands of years ago, but even of relatively modern cultures. Imagine for a moment, what would have remained of Ancient Egypt, if them had not engraved their stories and exploits on stone and monuments, the hardest witnesses of the human adventures.

In an era in which nothing is engraved in stone, and everything is so fragile that a simple power outage makes it inaccessible. What would our current civilization leave, which already lives more online than in person? More importantly, do we come to realize the unexpected turn that has accelerated in recent years? Because today, there is a powerful, indisputable stream, expanded to every application and messaging service, paradoxically called Story Mode. Ironic, that such a word is used for something designed and intended to disappear after just 24 hours.

What are we leaving aside when consuming and creating for such an ephemeral medium?

Persistent Memory

The global web does not have a unique, immovable form. It mutates over time and responds to the changes and needs of the society that uses it. For those born within their reach, it will be difficult to believe how different it was when it got to the uncontrolled, naive and innocent mass of the 90s.

Linked to exploitation by phone companies, who saw dial-up connections as a great way to hook up and then charge the equivalent of a call that could last for whole nights; The Internet grew from an active and pioneering minority to a community. In practice, there was nothing outside of what could be called as particularly authored, with the exception of the original professional pages of companies, more decorative than practical. Sites like GeoCities, with their neighborhoods and groups, where everyone had the possibility of being a webmaster of prehistory, with eternal gifs and an aesthetic that I will leave to the reader's comment, made school. These were times of learning, of debugging, that lasted for years, but also were never exempt from the slow walk towards the ephemeral.

It would be more than complicated today to find a good part of those areas that were, together with the first online forums, school and starting platform for the first generation to contact the Internet. They have vanished, leaving only their memory in the ether. Some of the most iconic remain as nostalgic ghosts, small time capsules suspended in a spider web of historical archives. At least, for now. Since nobody knows for sure when something like this can completely disappear. A clueless copyist, a lack of payment from the webmaster, or the absence on the plane of the living of anyone involved in saving such memory, and will be adrift.

The changing, economic and competitive condition of the Internet makes everything stored, displayed, accessible there, cost money. From web addresses to hosting, data quota and speed. All these things are totally unknown to the common user. That at most will have designed a web page in some kind of computer science class, but does not know all the other requirements that are there to make it public. In the face of such needs, the answer is apparently free solutions, but they sin from the fragility of their existence. Subject to the goodness or rather, to the ability to generate money from their owners by means of such a gift to their users.

Yes, putting a website online is something that costs money, time, effort and some expertise that, while accessible, is not innate. That is why services such as Facebook, Twitter or Instagram have been so successful: For making all this arcane part invisible to their users, that they never find out about such technical juggling behind the scenes. But there is also the seed of the ephemeral, as without the owners of such a platform, the same and all their content, can go into oblivion and fade into the ether. Just as thousands of neighborhoods, experiences and stories in GeoCities and so many other anonymous places of less relevance that have already been forgotten.

Strange irony of modernity, is that the aesthetics of those years has ended up being the inspiration for other generations that did not experience it, as is the case with the VaporWave. It seems that despite everything, the most persistent memory that the human has, is not the digital or magnetic, but the unconscious, collective. At least, while it lasts. For now.

WHO WILL READ WHAT IS WRITTEN IN WATER?

The fundamental thing to be able to read a story is that there is someone who writes it first. The endless quarry of characters that come and go throughout the centuries, is inexhaustible by itself. While there are humans there will be those who invent. In another order, a means of transmission is needed, be it oral, written, through words or stones. Coding and understanding such a code, for translation and subsequent interpretation, also seems paramount. Let us apply such a simple idea of communication to the Internet and our times.

Without a medium such as the network of networks, where everything lasts only the maintenance time given by its owners, there could be no such exchange. Our modern codices, hieroglyphs, or scrolls of the Dead Sea are volatile. Superfluous, fragile. With the disappearance, closure, fall or loss of such a digital file stored on servers, there is nothing that has the validity that the chiselled rock or the popular comment transmitted by generations has. Furthermore, the code created and employed by its users is so ephemeral that in less than a decade the leet (Internet slang), changes to the point of looking like a completely different language. There ends the possibility of getting the original message, an breaks. Sail adrift like a ghost ship that can't drop anchor on anyone who understands.

Perhaps for reasons like that, it is that in fact less and less is written on the Internet, and that always was little written to begin with. Author's blogs, with extensive and cerebral content, of long dimensions and coherence, are already a chimera of other times. Platforms like Twitter, of almost universal use, harshly punish the extension to the point of prohibiting it. No one seems to miss it or be annoyed from having to open tweet threads in order to express an idea, which could have been easily said in a sentence, without stopping to breathe. But this is not the fault of the medium, but a user's claim. If the Twitter model were bad, it would have failed. By continuing online, it validates in practice and with pure empiricism, the concept that users have progressively less to express, or do so in narrow characters. Same case can be seen on other social networks where it happens alike, even if there is not such a strict limit. There is no doubt: Collectively and for the universal success of these platforms, society writes and expresses itself less. To the point where it comes to take as an insult, a inconvenience, a challenge, reading or listening to someone explain on any subject extensively.

Censorship by extension, manifest or implied, is real. It is the counter face of a society that undoubtedly and by flow, raises its voice in a few characters, but it falls short then when consuming or taking the bate of command and having to use a generous extension of text. Thus losing, or at least relegating, a fundamental part of culture, the analytic, brainy, measured one. And all that by definition or form, cannot be summed up in a few words. Or that it shouldn't be synthesized. Can anyone imagine summing up several of the most verbose great masters like Tolstoy and his uncontainable, thirsty pen?

Modern social networks of exchange and information, human manifestations, do nothing more than prove the point. They are born, reversed and formed around a dogma of constant change. Of the ephemeral in all its power. In an Internet where things last little, the focus is to draw attention even in non-sancto ways, appealing to lying and misinformation as bait. For a matter of logic, in that mode, wins the immediate, the short, the abbreviated.

However, the issue does not stop there, but generates all an indigenous fauna and flora that preys on itself. Accomplished and important sites base their success on such an award of the "live and now". A true day-to-day industry, which also understands what its captive market demands. Because if, in addition, those who consume such information, seek it, and become addicted to the methodology. Seeing the stories with an expiration date of less than 1 day, goes from entertainment to necessity, as you can never know for sure what you may be missing from not doing so. Which leads to many conclusions and especially one question among many others.

In an age where the instant is king and demands constant attention, who will invest time into the great that deserves to be remembered into the future? Will it be paid attention, will it have its place, able to survive? Who will write the pages of the history we are living? If someone does it, let us hope it is not through states and stories that last less than 1 day, or depend on a backup that is present today, but tomorrow, we don't know.

THE WRONG IMMEDIACY

Such disposable current affairs that are consumed in a hurry, end up having an impact on media, content generators and, in a cause-effect feedback relationship, on the way of thinking of the public. It is much more important to be up-to-date, even if the data is unreliable, than to miss a follower or the chance to get on the social cart of a news story.

The lack of verification and objectivity, that used to be causal of dismissal and even of irreparable loss of prestige to a medium, no longer seems to be at all. In fact, such errors that are not, since they were avoidable from the outset, are justified by the failure of others, the fake news of the rival medium, or when not, completely ignored and without further mention.

To be fair, the reality is that beyond the methodological poverty implicit in such a dynamic, the multiplicity of voices currently being handled makes the work a real challenge. For professionals but also, for all other people, whether out of confidence or discouragement, or because of the impossibility at inverting the burden of proof, they cannot see clear which is the lie or truth. To separate the information from the unsubstantiated gossip.

The networks with their share of unproven, their character of easy erasure, their animadversion towards the eternal and infatuation with the fleeting; they do nothing but feed such miseries of verifiable thought. The same possibility that allows anyone with a camera and microphone to take on the role of a chronicler, generates a flow of errors and misdone interpretations, which forces a huge amount of time to be wasted on their checkup. Which is why such services, whether provided by social networks or by unscrupulous traditional media, prefer to ask forgiveness than ask permission.

Such a reality of information consumption could be limited to journalistic work, but it does not ends there at all. It only begins, and continues to move forward with post-truth analysis, untamed subjectivity, and the creation of increasingly watertight forms of thought, throughout society. The experts voice is lost, not because of their argumental failures, but by the waterfall of other opinions that cover it up. If we add to this the point already addressed of the extension, or the clear popularity of those who misinform from impunity, the cocktail becomes much more dangerous.

This is because our ways of consuming information directly affect our way of understanding, seeing, and comprehend the world around us. Making even more regrettable, the thought that much of that argument to see such world as it is comes from unversed data. Whether out of explicit hidden interest, or for innocent irresponsibility. Powerful and very dangerous tool that, we have already seen it, is used in the field of politics, news, and that has filtered into symbiosis with so many other and countless attitudes of daily life. One that more and more, rewards immediacy, speed, but also the wrong.

Story Mode

While the fragility of digital media can be traced back to its inception, the current prevailing model began its wanderings very slowly. Without fully understanding how or why. With a format that was more tending to be archived, but in turn, gradually enthroning the irrelevance of it. Focused on the now, rather than a sustained growth that could then be visited from posterity. The distant parents of the modern story mode.

With the advent of the Internet as a medium, communication tool and subsequent coronation as a modern deity, various services contributed their small grain of sand. Although sparsely related, places like Fotolog served to start making that concept of permanent assistance massive, with their solitary daily photo, and no more. The community that soon created itself in that network, which was among the 10 most visited in the world, would validate the model. Relating was no longer the only thing, and for that purpose Facebook would soon come taking giant steps. Meanwhile, another of the main perpetrators of the short, succinct, space-reduced feature, Twitter, began its wanderings around the world.

However, there was still a long time before both services became the mastodontic monsters they are today. In contrast, the beginning of Twitter was closer to shyness. Most of the people who became early adopters, pioneers of such a network, admitted at that time to not understand very well what it was about. Moreover, it was incredibly common that some of the early tweets, were about confusion or uncertainty about how or why to use Twitter. We are talking about the 2000-2010 decade, especially in the second part of it to be more precise. With countless fewer people than today and almost zero social penetration, being the exception some sociocultural groups or specific urban tribes, influenced by computer figures or gurus; the question was worth valid, logical. The ecosystem in which Twitter would then grow up was not yet there. But neither was the social need, nor the social adaptation to such an idea. These were still boom times on many blogs, and the famous and now almost archaic conception of Web 2.0,was still being written.

Many of these initial doubts would eventually disappear, exorcised by normality in vogue. Gradually, the Internet was no longer a place for a fairly specific social, economic and cultural sector. Beasts like YouTube broke in and brought an unknown massivity, a new capacity for entertainment and content creation that would eventually render obsolete its spiritual progenitor, the classic television model.

Much of the Internet's victory over such a television industry, with an economic power and the capability to generate almost unequivocal opinion as it used to have, came from the inclusion it promised. There was no need to wait, making times more flexible. It created a multiplicity of voices that otherwise could have never been expressed in a traditional medium, and raised new indigenous celebrities, such as those who still make daily income thanks to YouTube. There and at that moment much of the memes and videos that we keep referring to every now and then, were born. The change from viewer to be a part of, one of the banners of Internet 2.0, brought another logical consequence. Just as the voices multiplied, the material available thanks to that, exploded exponentially.

Human time, limited and finite, was simply insufficient to pay attention to all that nascent universe. As was the case with the Big Bang of cable television at its time, the number of eyes were not enough to see as much. In such overwhelming competition, the battle for mass attention may have germinated. One that continues to this day and that has clear winners: Those who bet on the content of shock, fast, impressive, but in turn also fallacious or fictional. In a format focused on being easily replicable, thus generating the necessary viralization, one of the objectives of each creator in the medium. Following almost the same steps that television had walked a couple of decades before, the goal was to get attention, and it didn't matter too much how it was achieved.

That need for enormous fame, ended up making obsolete the old saying that made reference to the 15 minutes of fame. If it were now 15 seconds, the truth is that perhaps we will exceed the number. Even worse, of relative fame, since with the multiplicity of new media, networks and formats for information, the ideal of a massive public that consumes more or less the same, has passed into history. Linguistic paradoxes aside, when it is internalized that the real, previous meaning of History and Story, refers to posterity, what remains forever. When today, it could not have taken a turn further from its origin.

THE ACCELERATION OF THE MODEL

It would come with the change of decade, and the subsequent unscheduled but expected obsolescence of the previous. The birth of networks like Instagram in 2010, although very different from the modern one and closer to a Fotolog without limits (or Flicker with a more social than professional component); Snapchat in 2011, which promoted the concept of disposable of what was shared there; and especially Vine, a short and gimmicky 7-second video service in 2013, would change the paradigm completely.

Each in its own way and at different times, influencing mutually and taking references from other smaller ones that have fallen into oblivion, helped to fertilize the ephemeral meadow of stories, states and updates that self-destruct after 1 day. While in other places of digital social exchange, such as Facebook, or content consumption, such as YouTube, the exposed had the possibility of staying there forever; not on these networks. There was the ability to do or expose more perennial things, without an expiration date, it is true. But the model clearly did not point that way. Whether by chance or causality, those same companies knew how to get, perhaps understand, the dynamics of the youth culture of their time. One based in effect, in the immediate, fleeting entertainment and that, without a doubt, rewarded brevity just like today.

The first generation fully born and raised in the Internet's time, knew what they wanted and how they wanted it. It had to be anonymous, either tacitly or explicitly, causing the original authorship to fall on completely irrelevant ground. To alleviate this, sites like Know Your Meme trace their origin, be it in video, images or phrases. It must also be ephemeral, part of a culture that in all its estates has a very accelerated useful life. Furthermore, and in consonance with the collective ideology that one could be a part, it was necessary to be able to replicate, go viral, share and insert itself into everyday life. Arriving at the point of uniting by the same action, filter or challenge people from very distant places and realities. An exemplary case of this we see in the Challenges like the famous Ice Bucket Challenge,

15

although the format has fallen into disuse with the passage of time. On the other hand, the massiveness, ubiquity and fame of the filters, states, stories, has only gone up and crossed the whole of society with the capacity for digital connection, which is no small feat.

The three major networks just mentioned, Instagram, Snapchat and Vine, were one to one reconverting to meet such uses and demands of youth culture. On their way, they ended up spreading such ideas to other older media, like Facebook, twinned seamlessly with the very heart of the short-lived pioneer, Twitter, and ended up creating a de facto standard that we can observe in its own way on TikTok, WhatsApp, Skype and as many social contact media there would be. The fast-consumption model, expired at the end of a given day or time, short and with viral goals, only needed the passage of years to become the king that it is today.

Those little moments of reality, daily life, broadcasting in minimal doses, have their own market and meaning beyond analysis. Although it is also worth asking, the real reason for choosing it as a medium, even when what its wanted to express is much longer, more extensive or complex. What is the point of making 50 micro stories, tweet threads or contiguous video chains, when the same information could have been much better structured and presented in different formats (column, article, video review, website, etc.)? Very simple: That the general public no longer reads or consumes the other formats. That making use of a superior media for such purposes, but which will have less impact, ends up defeating in the long run, the same communicational sense: Who wants to speak where they will not be heard?

As a link for broadcasting, these places with a transitory spirit soon became the audience, the preferred setting. It did not matter the nuisance of opening threads with few characters per tweet, concatenating videos that should have never been cut, or that there were already more consistent, serious, professional sites to broadcast. The mass, the common people, the massive public, did not go to those places. The tyranny of time, which applies to all things in human life, forced them to stay in those hunting grounds. The temptation to nest there, and the existential doubt not manifest of what could be lost by leaving the network of predilection, ended up winning. The source or the argument may reside there, yes; but the analytics on the pages are hard and real, the people who visit them rarely read everything. When not, they barely dive into the content by reading in a hurry, or without preamble, judging the argument by their knowledge or confidence in the reference site. A true fallacy of authority in full exercise, adapted to the digital world.

When in 2016 Vine, entirely under the control of Twitter, closed its possibility to upload new updates, the blow was more than given. It would be a matter of time for other competitors with similar and more applied ideas to micro-messaging, or the concept of social network, to raise the scepter and update it. The most similar and which coexisted with Vine was Snapchat. But it would be the giants like Instagram, Facebook and WhatsApp, from the same owner, who would popularize it among different age and social groups, massive in every sense of the word. They would no longer be the heritage of young people and in their use, those old memes and messages that have been replicating among adults, since the days of e-mail chains, would find a refuge. The Story Mode, had come to stay, and was everywhere.

THE QUESTION OF THE EPHEMERAL SPHINX
(BRIEF INTERLUDE)

Which is the animal with a voice that walks on four legs in the morning, wander in two in the afternoon, and three in the evening?

A contemporary Oedipus would answer: The same one which started studying with heavy Atlases and paper encyclopedias, then did it with educational software like Encarta, and now, studies with Wikipedia articles. Everything in the course of a generational day, or a life.

PYGMALION, OR ABOUT STILL LIFE

Art imitates life, and many times, life seems to emulate art. Something very similar could be said of the means of communication, interaction and coexistence that humans develop in various historical periods. This relationship of symbiosis between user and format is, in addition to logic, quite easy to understand when considering that the tools, limitations and communicational objectives of a particular era, go hand in hand. In short, we can communicate, in the ways we have available, and not in others. But also, in those that we most desire or best respond to our needs or will, whether they are knowable or unknown by ourselves.

As sculptors of our own interactions, those are subject to the inherent quality of the artists, their media and vision. We validate certain presentations, we consume specific opinions. By doing so, we encourage the issuer, as well as the medium that is in charge of transmitting, to be successful. Although we do not notice it, we also punish those who fall outside the aforementioned, with irrelevance, the mother of communication failure. The social networks we consume are nothing more than the living reflection of what our brains seem to like the most as a flock, at this precise moment in history. In the same way that happened before with television, radio or the written press. With the addictive additive, that effective feedback and measurement of the success and spread rate has never been faster and greater.

Like Ovid's Pygmalion, we are in love with our own creation. One that, basically, also owes its existence and with such configuration to that authorship. That it learns from us, that it could not have arisen in any other way than the one it is, because the tastes of the creator are what they are.

The logic supported by various studies indicate that the founders and developers of the ephemeral digital custom and its specific networks still understood, from a intuitive meaning, the importance of anxiety, a sense of belonging, and other various human mechanisms. If they didn't, they had to learn it fast, with the most accurate and tyrannical live monitoring system in history. They could not only listen to the complaints of their users, but also appreciate at what level various functions had an impact on the public. Both positive and negative, it should be clarified. Those who knew how to take advantage of that synergy and tame it, feeding the demands of the general public, amassed fortunes and relevance. Those that did not, fell into disuse or niche stagnation. A strange case of collective democracy, in which you vote with your presence, and in esoteric ways for the common people who, even in our era of so much transparency, do not know how to interpret code or the whole thing behind the scenes that a web based service implies. Another great difference with the previous eras, when the Internet was the land of experts and neophytes, who soon learned the almost arcane secrets of html.

It is easy to judge from a distance, like someone who has nothing to do with the matter, the miseries of digital modernity. However, it is much more complex, and undoubtedly revealing, to understand that there was no other obscure hand handling the threads of the Internet puppet and its customs, than that of its users. Perhaps there were others, but the incontestable validation or denial came from them. This can be witnessed by several companies such as Microsoft or Google, which despite having virtually unlimited monetary and technical resources, had their own failures with millions of losses. Case of Skype and its fall into disuse, or that of Google+, a platform that had to be finally abandoned. When the digital society lowers its thumb, there is no millionaire company that can convince it otherwise.

The social rupture generated by virtuality reaches such a point that in truth, one cannot stop thinking if in the end, rather than in front of a sculpture, a piece of our creation but different, we are not in front of a mirror. One that enhances beauties and accentuates imperfections, for those who want to see them. A not so still life, very alive and constantly changing, which is too similar to its creators.

DISPOSABLE LIFE

The biggest clue that the Internet changes and mutates with us, instead of being a capricious entity that grows at pleasure, is given by other customs and human means that have also led the helm towards the same coasts. Without going too far in anthropological, philosophical analyzes of society itself, but in the same neighborhood: that of technology.

The gradual volatility of the memories, capacities, processors and microchips, as well as the programs, functions or media they generate, are not new. It is a slow process that has been going on for decades, that responds to an infinity of reasons and causes, from the globalized economy, to the increase in people and, therefore, users and buyers inhabiting the planet. Even taking everything into account, it is not enough to understand the forced ephemeral condition of cell phones, computers, the cult of the latest or programmed obsolescence. One that to make matters worse, is too close in time.

At an age when we could well afford excellent products with five-year durability and uninterrupted use, we do just the opposite. Although the construction materials allow it in the smartphone market, to take an emblematic example, none with 2 or 3 years old continues to perform in the same way. The ecosystem is advancing so fast and it needs to do so to maintain the inertia of purchase, that in the established time period, infinity of cameras will come out, promises of folding, multiplication of RAM. The curious thing is that the public, whether due to fetishism, a sense of belonging or advertising conviction, endorses it. Although their minds and mouths say one thing in the comments, their pockets still pay. When you want to be able to interpret with rigor, actions always speak louder than sayings.

Under the label of progress, although it is not well known to where the progress is being made, or what for, such foundations of expiration are hidden. As the leaves of deciduous trees in the fall season rush to the ground, so do bills, physical or digital, fall to change the twilight lifespan of new technologies. Incidentally, this time we are passing has also raised the volatility of the means of payment or currencies, embodied in entities with a nominal market value as restless as the sea. Bitcoin, Ethereum and other currencies that will never know the coin format, ironic as it sounds, are the economic representatives of a period where even money can go from being worth to not doing so.

The human beings, who previously could have evaded such conditions and turn to safety or the most stable, now instead chooses of their own free will to enter the maelstrom. No, without a doubt it is no coincidence at all the ephemeral configuration that can be seen. Rather, it responds to the own concerns and desires of the collective unconscious, larger, global and more changing than ever. A consistent technology, expanding relentlessly in both idea and form, ubiquitous to the point of being almost universal, is the result.

To appreciable phenomena such as the increase in garbage worldwide, and the need for recycling, not as an ethical-moral decision, but rather from the imperative for well-being; the obvious applications of the same philosophy in the field of digital are added. The parallelism by emulation and contagion, is evident in many planes of modern life, too much crossed by applied science. Media as simple in appearance as photography used to be, have changed their interaction with the user, to the point where they can no longer dispose of them in a physical album, but instead become a property and remain under the tutelage of some online company. The same thing happens at different levels with other arts and customs that are daily in today's human being.

The incredible thing is that even the required speed of adaptation to changes, which was already fast, has accelerated. Applications, digital services, specific interactions between users of various media, also gadgets or devices to access them, are fleeting. They do not last or become persistent over a single generation or age range. That characteristic process of contemporary life, appreciated since the Industrial Revolution, exacerbated with the change to the 20th century and its scientific advances, has only spiraled upward since the advent of the Internet and home computing. The great game changers, generators of hinge moment in the historical section that we have to live, but we rarely get to understand.

Mastodons such as the old Messenger, IRC, ICQ, Facebook that as a platform is falling, the already named GeoCities, Fotolog, Vine and many others, today are seen as heritage of the past. The massiveness and impressive penetration they used to have did not save them from a stormy runaway riverbed, the one which modern technology and its forgotten paladins has. Some who knew how to be so well-known, used, accepted, that it is hard to really believe, that they no longer exist or their importance lies more as a conglomerate, the case of Facebook. How then, can we expect interaction with the devices used, in effect, to access such media? Ephemeral. With a fairly young expiration date, this is how we create cell phones, computers, televisions. Yes, there is a clear component from the construction of such, that for the required amount and perhaps for the convenience of the companies, they should last a suggested time, and no more. But the foundation and reflections in other parts of society, their ways of buying, consuming and relating, are also there.

PROGRAMMED FRAGILITY

When the force of nature is too great, other things just flow with it. Like those that are washed away in waves and tides, or those that fly in the midst of storms and hurricanes. What is the point of opposing a force of this magnitude? The same question has been asked and answered, regarding the volatility of the digital world, by the people and companies that inhabit it.

Far from looking for some kind of posterity, even the code that gives them life is thought of constant metamorphosis. The transition from Flash to Java and more recently Html5, are a new way to leave thousands of applications and products in obsolescence. Unprotected against the attack of hackers and therefore, meaningless in a fully computerized society and that maintains with certain conscious zeal their private data, although later is given away by accepting a section of terms and conditions.

Nothing ever sees a final edition. As well as a good part of the development that was previously internal, behind the closed doors of the company, and with a good filter of tests before seeing the light of the public, now it is later in its entirety. This last point is especially noticeable in the video game industry, however, it is already common in all those that require interaction or feedback with the end user. As everything is connected if we analyze enough, we will find that one of the reasons for this is, in effect, the variable and immense offer of the market with respect to the physical, hardware. Challenge that force developers to adapt their creations for various media, systems, languages and environments where those must perform later. The lack of a unique means for programming or designing, and the explicit need to keep it updated for the new generations that come out with a difference of weeks or months, and not years like a few decades ago, feeds the collective monster of modernization.

From the side of the devices that allow us to exercise this present, smartphones, computers, connected televisions, something very similar happens. With the small difference that every so many years, the industry of such seems to impose, or respond to the popular clamor as you want to understand, some new gadget, function or improvement. That, despite having been expendable until the moment of its creation, from it becomes a necessity. Resisted at first, with doubts from the general public, over time, reviews and adaptation, upon payment by the consumer of course, ends up turning commonplace. The simple and perfect example could be the already not-so-modern of the multitude of cameras in the telephones, the ports of charge and audio that leave decades of previous development obsolete by force, or the folding capacity of the screens.

Industry, developers and buyers all seem to go to the same place, either of their own free will or drawn by a current of change too powerful to successfully oppose. As is the case with the stream of the great planetary wills, although in private many people denounce certain boredom stemming from having to think about changing things so quickly, or come to the brutal honesty of admitting anger at it; The companies that are leading the way in that direction are still the most successful and current of all. The flow of money does not stop. Thus, the model is validated.

Perhaps, for some kind of prudence. Understanding that in a world with disposable equipment, short life spans and forced updates, the only thing left to change and be replaced is the very user. That must adapt in record speed to keep up with the circumstances and not be passed over, left behind, replaced. For now, so far.

From Ephemeral to Instantaneous

The reigning modality today. The one that moves young masses and confirms a good part of the hypothesis; in addition to having all chances on becoming even stronger in the near future. The one that came when the technical capacity allowed to reach the point, before unthought, of being able to broadcast live from one's own home, instead of doing it in the environment of a closed television studio. But also, the most tyrannical regarding time. So much, that it requires a devotion from both those who create it and those who consume it. A cult that creates expressions, colloquial culture and helps to fill infinity of missing roles in the youngest, also bringing with it innumerable new dynamics and problems.

Heirs, spiritual brothers of the previous Podcasts, grandchildren in turn in some strange form of the classic radio format. The genealogies of the live video broadcast, available to a horde of independent creators, is one that follows the DNA of the Internet to the letter. A logical evolution that was hidden, denied behind the lack of means. Until these, in the form of web cameras, microphones and stable Internet connections, were present.

Modern electrical empires have risen or been forced to evolve upon their arrival. This was the case with Justin.Tv, later converted into the best-known Twich, and YouTube, which now allows the same possibility of transmitting as another service. Of looser content, usually framed in entertainment, or the punctual realization of something. Of what? Well, that is left to the originality, tastes and will of the issuer. From video game professionals practicing, competing or enjoying themselves, to people who dance, share their day to day, chat with their visitors, or basically anything. There are not many limits, except the obvious, logical ones that come when analyzing the medium, and its consequences. Because the same condition that makes it so accessible, requires instead a sacrifice, that of time.

Lacking a script, being chaotic and without a predetermined purpose, which if ever, expands, delays, adds up towards new frontiers. They are consumed and feel like a dose of synthetic everyday and real life. Just as if the viewer were accompanying the streamers in their work from the same place, in their bedroom, studio or living room. That real life-like closeness, which transpires from the same casual posture, and in appearance, without masks from the creator of the show, can last from a few minutes, to hours. Many, countless hours, thanks in part to another special feature of the medium, the instant rating effect. The one that allows followers to be added at various times to the transmission, and not from the beginning.

A very hand-picked, personal format, in which to know what happened, you had to be there. Every and all the time. Paying attention. Where now and again, moments of interest are taken and supported in a more lasting way, although just as volatile if we think about the long term. In reality, these video summaries are just a transfer from an immediate medium to an ephemeral one. Curious way of defining the phenomenon, the evolution of the transitory, to the instantaneous, and back to the previous medium.

If we reflect on the fact that this type of consumption of information, entertainment and even news is incredibly popular among the youngest, we will understand that the model can only continue to grow. Until, perhaps, an even more demanding and fleeting one replaces it, or expands it. Or their own consumers look for something, if possible, more immediate.

Lost Footprint

A few years ago, with the change of decade and the first steps of the 2010s, conclusions began to be drawn, to generate thoughts and analysis regarding the recent past. The Internet was no longer a novelty and showed that it was not going to go anywhere, but rather to deepen its transversality and range of action. In relationships, families, love, human possibilities, work. In everything. One of the notable concepts, very typical of that time, was that of Digital Fingerprint or Shadow. Image that explored the brand that we were leaving on our tour, the trail of our ship to surf the web.

Marked by the awakening that involved recognizing the steps taken, that footprint recorded on the net brought back memories and in many cases shame. When not also, problems, due to conflicts between offline life and anonymity, conceptual grays or even legal, typical of another era. One in which the Internet was still seen a little, like a game. A curiosity that was accessible and perhaps, like so many other fashions or human gadgets, would not last long. But oh it lasted, boy did it really.

When encountering the specter of the past self, represented in posts, photos, articles, profiles and other digital media, the experience was not always a good one. In fact, one of the reasons why the notion of trace or fingerprint began to be thought, was given by theorizing how much time passed before things were deleted from the Internet. A very big problem for those burdened by scammers, who saw their data or privacy leaked on the web, against their will or with little foresight consent.

From a more technical point of view, the Digital Footprint referred to and refers to the security, tracking and authoring devices, depending on the case, that allows to single out files, creators, consumers. Various purposes aim to create such a network of personal individualization, of evidence and cross-data, often used to safeguard the same security of online users against malicious characters. Or to generate an efficient means of governmental, state, and social persecution. As with so many other human tools, everything depends on the context, the objectives, opinions. But the truth is that the means exist, just as there is very little real anonymity on the Internet. Each click can be traced if wanted, especially that of a user who is not an expert in computer security, a category in which the vast majority of people fall. Cases of massive online surveillance come to light from time to time to confirm that the interest in everyone's digital lives exists. One more reason to understand the Cyber Shadow as a trace that, if necessary can also be seen, as the track the hunters follows to find their prey.

Since then, various sites, services and applications have tried to give users the ability to hide or keep their online actions private. Public awareness, cases of cyber abuse or scam with media repercussions, had a powerful influence on this. Especially when society began to see that the Internet was not some kind of virtual alternate reality, but that what was happening there could well transpire and generate influence from the other side of the screen, in the real world. We can even risk saying that it began to be understood that in fact the virtual was also real. It was only backed in another format.

The pendulum swung once more and crossed from one end to the other. From the times when nobody feared for anonymity, to some intermediate caution. In which many of us grew up under the recommendation never to show our face or real names (empirical origin of nicknames or monikers); to a new era in which the name, among the sea of people that swarms the Internet, is almost anecdotal. The influence of sites like Facebook, where being the same person online as in everyday life, responded to the function of being found later by friends and family, was fundamental. The massiveness with which that happened, and the communication advantages that its users experienced, made the fear disappear permanently. The promise that perhaps, with luck and effort, they could capitalize or even acquire a certain fame through these means, using their own name as a personal brand, convinced the rest. Today, that the Digital Fingerprint is bigger, more exact and visible, it is when it matters least to the common people.

Perhaps that is why we do not finish to understand that a good part of such cybernetic mark that we are leaving, the trail behind us that testifies to the past presence is, even with all that said, an ephemeral mark written in the liquid of modern society. It may be easier than ever to follow it for governments and agencies for various purposes, it is true. But for the common, individual human, limited in resources, there is a whole technical veil difficult to pierce. A lack of appreciation in the importance of what these data, so interesting for companies and analysts, can actually mean. But above all things, a total ignorance on the level of fragility that is managed in everything supported by those mediums.

How many family albums have disappeared with an error, user deletion or administrator censorship? What amount of stories, tales, letters written in a few lines between famous people and personalities, will not reach the history halls, since they will be erased before? Does anyone realize that a government decision, a blockage or update to the terms of service, can take away from us part of our Digital Footprint? Both the accidental, the unwanted, and the intended, the one that shows us a part of our own life. The one we live through crossed by networks. Of which it is very possible, little and nothing remains with time. It remains to wonder what we would know of the past, of the remote and not so ephemeral times, if their tracks had been as volatile as ours.

IRONIC EXPIRATION

All these edges of the perishable reality that we have to live in, are in addition to what is stated, contradictory. We do not live in a primitive, remote age, where accessing a certain aspiration for digital immortality is impossible. The ancients, despite their infinite technical limitations, were able to leave us a good part of their culture. Their stories, myths and cosmogony. It is true that accidentally, through such disparate means as a piece of art decorating a vessel. But they stayed. Be it in Dead Sea scrolls, paintings on the walls or frozen in the ashes of Pompeii. If our backups are only digital, in 1000 years, when the life expectancy of all the hard drives or computer systems has been exceeded 100 times. What will remain?

For reasons ranging from economic to industrial, perhaps computational progress, we have immersed ourselves in the liquid times that Bauman wrote about. We have spiralized, accelerated them. Without stopping to think about what we are leaving on the road to adopt and walk such a path towards immateriality. The fantasy of thinking that in many places the same information is stored as there is on the Internet, gives us as a society a security that is not so accurate. There are many things that are not achieved or have never been achieved online. Others, that by decision of a government, censorship or change of epoch, may fall into the dangerous terrain of disappearance. We must never forget that, added to the natural disasters that overwhelmed it, the multiple times that the Library of Alexandria was burned or destroyed, they have mostly political, religious overtones.

The same era in which there is more accessibility, more capacity to generate media and perennial interactions, is the one that is most committed to an immediate model. One that from technique to attitude, hardware to its use, are volatile. Feasible of failure. And nobody seems to care much about it. Saint Cloud, is prayed to as if it were an infallible way of support, when in truth it is not. It is only a service that depends on an infinity of factors to be operational, subject to legal norms and conditions of service, which, as they clarify, may vary or fail.

The same modality is replicated in all levels, the univocal, unquestionable format. We live in times where nothing is certain, and everything can be criticized in the short term. Betting on immediacy and escaping to posterity as if it were a compulsion, systematically, is our tricked, suggested possibility. But also the one that offers the most momentary success, the greatest penetration in the new generations. Whoever does not follow the pattern is exposed to falling into irrelevance, condemned like everyone else, to living alone in the time given. What would have become of the great universal masters, so fascinated with the idea of surviving and defeating death and time from their art, their craft, their life drive, in our transitory days?

The passing of the years may seem ruthless, but it is usually fair. Those who play all their opportunities in the immediate, the gimmicky, end up being relegated when the social and cultural turns change. Sites like Internet Archive try to give their share of immortality to the medium. But even they depend on technical availability, which keeps the entire Internet alive, to continue existing. Their servers are not maintained based on good thoughts or magical realities typical of silicon. They must be governed by the legal regulations of distribution in force in the countries that host the site's servers. As with any other digital thing that we access without understanding how.

It is a true irony, although understandable, the one resulting from the idea that the medium which less deterioration of the original material delivers, in turn, is the one that can make it disappear completely at once. Without possibility of salvage. Much more prone to failure than we are willing to admit.

Until Then

In conclusion, it is not the objective of this writing to fall into cheap tremendousness and caustic criticism. Both are ultimately unproductive and short-sighted. It does not present a destructive view of the prevailing model, but rather accuses some of its most obvious shortcomings and vulnerabilities. But above all, it tries to bring into the light such defects and looks towards the immediate, to call for the necessary reflection, nowadays so neglected in pursuit of evanescent effect.

It can be argued against the apparent, that most of the issues discussed here come from many decades ago. That the gradual and total abandonment of the media, including its replacement by others that were also substituted later; it is a dynamic typical of modern life. On the contrary, the objective is to bring to consciousness just that, which is a mechanism already known, perfectible. However, not only do we not abandon or take it into account, but to top it off, we are accelerating decade by decade, lustrum by lustrum, year by year, month by month.

The spiral becomes every time faster and with each revolution sideways, many fall outside and are forgotten. Pieces of culture that disappear from all traces to be left only in the memories of those who lived it. Condemned to obsolete reproduction formats and that, if they do not have some kind of adaptation in the inter-generational gap, will be the pasture of total oblivion. It is not guesswork or divinatory art, it happens and has happened even with great references of culture, with books, movies, series and other media that we now only have mention of.

The internet and digitization can have promises of eternity, only if their guardians are able to keep them. Sites fallen into disgrace like MegaUpload or Rapidshare bear silent witness to it. Just like any other of the countless places already lost in the sands of cyber time. Place where, more and more, the actual prevails. That which produces shock, and the momentary. Where in a rare opportunity, and on fewer occasions, it is thought or produced thinking of the long term, the future, to build for posterity.

What can perhaps be taken as a claim of an old folk, unsuited to the new generations. In love with abandoned times and formats, digital romantic of the networks and the historical moment that he had to live. Some of that may be. But if it happens to me, it is sure that those who today sit on the crest of the wave, will feel it even stronger. Those who believe they have tamed or become accustomed to its whirling upward speed. Those who dance contentedly to the tune of programmed fragility and live without leaving a footprint that tells their path. Those who prefer to be wrong fast, than sure and well informed in time. Those who do not read, because such a medium is reserved for things that aspire to a certain future, but in turn only consume liquid media, and nobody writes in water. Someday, sooner rather than later, such assurances may fail, flop, and find no record of their passage on this plane, or something that future generations will remember of them. Until then, they will feel invincible, in vogue, without noticing that even that feeling of eternal change is perishable.

It is certain that the tools we have are the best, most efficient, decentralized and with the greatest scope in history. Still, that doesn't hide their intrinsic fragility, their limited access by many factors. Nor should the concept of producing specifically for them enchant us, approaching step by step the expiring. By using them, the modern human being must learn to remember the long term more often. The posterity. Because there are no aspirations of immortality or memories, for those who live in the eternity of an ephemeral age.

CONTENTS